Junella

MW01537373

I hope thet 1994
Brings luck & laughter
the whole year through.

Yvonne Dufelt - Mogul Welborn
Dec 20, 1995

#64

HEART MEMORIES

A Book Of Poems By:
Yvonne Dufek-Hogue Welborn

**Produced in association with
Northwoods Press**

COPYRIGHT PAGE

HEART MEMORIES: A Book of Poetry. Copyright by Yvonne Dufek-Hogue Welborn. No part of this book can be reproduced in any manner including, stored in a retrieval system, electronic, mechanical, photocopying, recording or transmitted in any other way. Without the written permission of the Author and Publisher. Inquries should be addressed to: CAL'S Personal Printing, P.O. Box 298, Thomaston, Maine 04861. (207) 832-6665

Library of Congress catalog card number: 95-72712.

**Produced in association with
Northwoods Press
P. O. Box 298
Thomaston, ME 04861**

DEDICATION

I dedicate this book to two people. First my sister Loraine McKenna
and the poem A LITTLE OLD LADY. Without her believing in me this book
wouldn't of been possible. I also dedicate this book in Loving Memory of my
Father Louis J. Dufek and the poem HE WAS THERE. He was the greatest Father
anyone could ever have.

A PERSONAL STATEMENT

I am a poet. I enjoy writing and expressing myself through words. I feel the Poetry I have written will provide many readers with enjoyable reading. I hope it will open their minds to new ideas and ways of expressing themselves to others. I feel anyone can write a book. Just believe in yourself, have patience and let the thoughts and words come freely. Then the Poem or Story will ease out for the world to read.

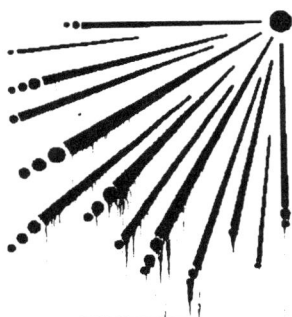

EXCERPT

Our tomarrows may never come
So we must do what we can
      Before the setting sun...
Live each and every moment we can
For our lives will be fullfilled now and then...
Live, Love, Laughter too
Let's let all this come shinning through...

TABLE OF CONTENTS

TABLE OF CONTENTS

INTRODUCTION

Heart Memories is Yvonne Dufek-Hogue Welborn's first book of Poetry. However she has been writing poetry for eighteen years. She has had several poems published in Books by The National Library of Poetry in 1994 and 1995. She had a Poem called " MY POP " PUBLISHED IN THE YPSILANTI PRESS in 1978. Yvonne is a member of the International Society of Poets.

HEART MEMORIES

A LITTLE OLD LADY

A LITTLE OLD LADY OLD AND GRAY

SITTING IN HER CHAIR FROM DAY TO DAY...

WATCHING AND WAITING FOR HER SONS TO COME

CALLING THEIR NAMES ONE BY ONE...

HER YESTERDAY HAS COME AND GONE

SHE REMEMBERS ONLY TODAY AND THE SETTING
SUN...

SHE WATERS HER PLANTS AND WATCHES THEM GROW

NOT CARING HOW SHE IS GROWING OLD...

SHE GREETS HER VISITORS AS IF THEY WERE GOLD

SHE ASK YOU TO STAY FOR AWHILE IN HER FOLD...

CHIT CHAT AND OLD STORIES TOLD...

SHE SITS IN HER ROCKER AND PRAYS

VISIT AGAIN AND A LITTLE LONGER STAY...

HE WAS THERE

WHEN I WAS BORN I HAD

JUST ONE SPECIAL WONDERFUL DAD...

HE WAS THERE WHEN I WAS SMALL

HE WAS THERE WHEN I GREW TALL...

HE WAS THERE WHEN I WAS A CHILD

HE WAS VERY GENTLE AND MILD...

HIS LAP WAS MY FAVORITE PLACE TO BE

WHILE HE SANG HIS SONGS AND ROCKED
ME...

HE WAS THERE WHEN I NEEDED A FRIEND

HE WAS THERE EVEN TO THE END...

HE WAS THERE WHEN I NEEDED HIM SO

HE RARELY EVER TOLD ME NO...

HE WAS THERE AT NIGHT

HE WAS THERE EVEN WHEN IT WAS BRIGHT...

MY DAD LOUIS J. DUFEK WAS ALWAYS NEAR

I AM THANKFUL HE WAS, HE WAS SO DEAR...

PEACE ON OUR EARTH

LETS TRY TO SAVE THE EARTH FOR THREE

LETS PRESERVE THE AIR AND STOP CUTTING DOWN THE TREE...

CRIMES AND KILLING ARE RUINING THE EARTH

LETS HAVE PEACE ON OUR EARTH LIKE IT WAS AT IT'S BIRTH...

PEOPLE ALL AROUND THE LAND

SHOULD PRESERVE THE PEACE, NO MATTER IF YOUR WHITE, BLACK OR TAN...

OUR EARTH IS FOR ALL NATIONALITIES TO SHARE

SO LETS ALL PITCH IN FOR PEACE AND FRESH AIR...

LOVE AND UNITY IS DYING FAST

LETS HAVE PEACE BEFORE IT WILL PASS...

WAR, POLLUTION, NUCALUR AIRFARE

IS KILLING OUR PEOPLE ON A DARE...

WE NEED TO FIGHT FOR WHAT WE NEED

PEACE, CARING, UNITED IN OUR WORLD INDEED...

PEACE ON EARTH FOR EVERYONE

FOR OUR MOTHERS, FATHERS, DAUGHTERS AND SONS...

LETS STOP THE BLOOD SHED AND LEARN TO LOVE

SO EVERYONE CAN FEEL AT PEACE LIKE THE DOVE...

LETS HURRY QUICK, LETS HURRY FAST

BEFORE OUR EARTH IS DESTROYED AT LAST...

THE MIRROR

THROUGH GODS IMAGES THE REFLECTIONS I SEE

WHAT COULD IT BE, WHAT COULD IT BE

WHAT'S IN THAT MIRROR LOOKING BACK AT ME...

IT DOES EXACTLY WHAT I DO

IT HOLD IT'S ARM JUST LIKE ME TOO...

THE MIRROR IS SOMETHING MAGIC BY FAR

SOMETIMES IT'S BRIGHT, SOMETIMES LIKE TAR...

THE MIRROR IMAGE OF THE PERSON

COULD BE A POLICE, TEACHER OR SOMEONE NURSING...

SOMEONE RICH, POOR, WHITE OR BLACK

AND WHEN I TURN AROUND MY BACK...

THE MIRROR IMAGE CATCHES THAT TOO

IMAGES OF ME AND YOU...

WHAT IS LOVE

LOVE IS TWO PEOPLE HOLDING HAND

DOING FOR EACH OTHER ALL THEY CAN...

EYES THAT SAY SO VERY MUCH

OR THAT VERY SPECIAL TOUCH...

HONESTY, SINCERE AND CARING

HELP EACH OTHER AND SHARING...

CANDLE LIGHT DINNERS AT NIGHT

JUST TWO PEOPLE UNDER THE MOON LIGHT...

THOSE SPECIAL MOMENTS JUST FOR TWO

EACH TIME FEELS BRAND NEW...

GOD GIVES ALL OF THIS TO PEOPLE IN LOVE

TO HOLD ONTO, BUILD UPON AND TO KEEP NEW...

JUST WALK IN LOVE

IF YOU WANT TO BE ACCEPTED

WALK IN LOVE...

IF YOU WANT TO BE MY FRIEND

WALK IN LOVE...

IF YOU WANT PEACE

JUST WALK-WALK- WALK IN LOVE...

IF YOU WANT SOMEONE TO LOVE YOU

WALK IN LOVE...

IF YOU WANT FORGIVENESS

WALK IN LOVE...

THEN THE WORLD WILL WALK WITH YOU

IF YOU JUST WALK-WALK-WALK IN LOVE...

IF YOU WANT HAPPINESS

WALK IN LOVE...

IF YOU WANT YOUR HEART FILLED

WALK IN LOVE

JUST WALK-WALK-WALK IN LOVE...

LOVE IS

LOVE IS CARING

LOVE IS KIND...

LOVE IS SHARING

LOVE IS BLIND...

LOVE IS ENSURING

LOVE IS ENDURING...

LOVE IS GIVING

LOVE IS RECEIVING...

LOVE IS YOU

LOVE THAT'S SO TRUE...

SPECIAL LOVE

THE LOVE WE HAVE EXPERIENCE IS SPECIAL,YOU KNOW

AS OUR LOVE COMES OUT OF US AND GROWS...

THE SPECIAL WAY WE SAY THINGS AND WRITE

MAKES OUR HEARTS, BODIES SING AT NIGHT...

LOVE IS SPECIAL THAT WE KNOW

LIKE STARS IN OUR EYES THAT GLOW...

THROUGH PEN AND PAPER WE HAVE SAID A LOT

THE LOVE AND TENDERNESS WE SHARE AND GOT...

NO MAN OR WOMAN CAN TAKE FROM US

THE LOVE WE HAVE WITHIN AND TRUST...

WITH YOUR LOVE WITHIN ME, AND MINE IN YOU

OUR SPECIAL LOVE WILL ALWAYS   FEEL LIKE NEW...

I WANT TO YELL, SCREAM AND SHOUT

AND LET THIS LOVE COME ON OUT...

BUT ONY TO ONE PERSON IN THE WORLD FOR ME

AND THAT PERSON IS: YOU, YOU SEE...

YES OUR LOVE IS SPECIAL LOVE

BROUGHT TO US BY THE ANGELS ABOVE...

THE LOVE OF

YOU HAVE FILLED MY HEART WITH LOVE

SO PURE AND BRIGHT LIKE A MORNING DOVE...

YOU HAVE MADE MY LIFE COMPLETE

I LOVE YOU HONESTY, YOU'RE NEAT...

YOUR LOVE HAS PUT SMILES ON MY FACE

MADE MY WORLD A HAPPY PLACE...

I HAVE SEARCHED ON SEA AND LAND

AND FOUND MY HANDSOME, GOOD LOOKING MAN...

YOUR WORDS OF LOVE MAKE MY HEART GLOW

AS EACH PASSING DAY OUR LOVE IT DOES GROW...

YOUR SMILING FACE IN MY MIND IS RADIANT AND BRIGHT

WITH YOUR LOVE IN MY LIFE, MY DARK DAYS ARE ALWAYS LIGHT...

THANKS MY GUY FOR BEING JUST YOU

OUR LOVE IS BRIGHT AND NEW...

I LOVE YOU, YOU'RE EVERYTHING TO ME

AND I LOVE YOU, HONESTLY...

ANGELS

ANGELS, ANGELS EVERYWHERE

DO I LOOK, DO I DARE...

IF I SEE THEM WILL THEY BE

LOOKING RIGHT AT ME...

EVERYWHERE THAT I GO

MY GUARDIAN ANGEL IS IN TOW...

WHEN IT'S DARK AND I AM IN FRIGHT

I CALL MY ANGEL TO HELP ME, THROUGH THE NIGHT...

ANGELS ARE MESSENGERS FROM GOD TOO

WHEN GOD CAN'T COME ANGELS DO...

WHEN YOUR IN NEED OR IN PAIN

CALL UPON YOUR ANGEL AND YOU WILL GAIN...

YOU WILL BE HEALTHY AND HAPPY TOO

KNOWING YOUR ANGEL IS AROUND WAITING FOR YOU...

TRUST THE LORD

PUT YOUR TRUST IN THE LORD

THEN YOU WONT HAVE TO WORRY NO MORE...

TRUST HIM AND HE WILL DO HIS BEST

TO EASE YOUR PAIN AND PUT YOU AT REST...

GOD HELPS US WHEN WE ARE DOWN

DON'T PUSH HIM AWAY OR YOU MAY DROWN...

THE BIRDS, THE ANIMALS, THE TREES TOO

ARE KISSES FROM GOD FROM THEE TO YOU...

THE DEW ON FLOWERS EARLY IN THE DAY

ARE KISSES FROM GOD AND THAT'S HIS WAY...

I KNOW THE LORD ABOVE

WILL SHINE DOWN TO ME WITH HIS LOVE...

SO I WON'T WORRY ALL THE TIME

I WILL LET GOD KNOW WHAT'S ON MY MIND...

I FEEL AT EASE, I FEEL AT REST

CAUSE I TRUST THE LORD TO DO HIS BEST...

LET GOD IN YOUR LIFE

LEAVE YOUR LIST OF TROUBLES TO GOD

WHEN YOU GO TO SLEEP DON'T WORRY, SLEEP LIKE A LOG...

SLEEP COMES EASY WHEN YOU TRUST

THE BRAIN DON'T HAVE TO WORRY AND RUST...

WHEN GOD IS IN YOUR HEART AND SOUL

IT'S A GREAT FEELING THAT YOU KNOW...

LIFE AND WORRIES OF EVERY DAY

DON'T SEEM SO BAD AND GO AWAY...

GOD LOVES EVERYONE EACH DAY

EVEN THE ONES WHO NEVER PRAY...

WITH GOD IN YOUR LIFE EVERYTHING IS FINE

BETTER THAN ALL THE GOLD IN A MINE...

GOD WONT LET YOU DOWN WHEN YOUR POOR

LIKE FRIENDS, FAMILY DO AND SHOW YOU THE DOOR...

HIS LOVE IS GOOD AND EVER LASTING AND NEW

LET GOD IN YOUR LIFE AND YOU WILL BE HAPPY TOO...

GODS CREATIONS

GOD CREATED THE TREES

THE BROWN, GREEN,RED AND ORANGE LEAVES...

THE RIVERS HOW BEAUTIFUL THEY FLOW

THE WINDS OH HOW THEY BLOW...

THE SINGING OF THE BIRDS TOO

ARE GODS CREATION FOR YOU...

CATAPILLERS ~~CRAWKUBGM FRIGS CRIAJUBG~~ CRAWLING Frogs CRoaKing
FISH IN PONDS SOAKING...

CRICKETS SINGING THEIR PRETTY TUNES

WHILE WATER FOWL SWIMMING LIKE LOONS...

SPIDERS CREATING PRETTY WEBS

OR HEARING THE ECHO OF THE EBB...

FIRE FLIES AT NIGHT

LIGHTING THE SKIES SO BRIGHT...

GOD CREATES ALL OF THIS AND MORE

IF ONLY WE OPEN OUR EYES AND THE DOOR...

GODS CREATIONS ARE THE BEST TOO

FROM GOD AND HIS LOVE, FOR ME AND YOU...

SMILES FROM GOD

EVERY DAY WE GET SMILES FROM GOD

LIKE THE GREE, GREEN SOD...

THE BEAUTIFUL BLUE SKIES ABOVE

WHERE BIRDS FLY WITH WINGS OF LOVE...

THE BARK AND LEAVES OF THE TREE

THAT PROVIDES SHADE FOR YOU AND ME...

THE RIVERS AND STREAMS THAT FLOW THROUGH

TO HELP MAKE OUR WORLD FRESH AND NEW...

FLOWERS WITH THE MORNING DEW

ARE KISSES FROM GOD FROM ME TO YOU...

ANIMALS OF ALL SPECIES AND KINDS

HELPS TO BRING PEACE TO OUR MINDS...

RAIN HELPS TO NEXTRALIZE THE LAND

SO GODS PEOPLE HAVE A PLACE TO STAND...

RAINBOWS ARE SMILES FROM GOD

MAKE SURE TO SEE THEM AND NOD...

GIVE THANKS FOR EVERYTHING YOU SEE

CAUSE THESE ARE SMILES FROM GOD TO THEE...

PEN FRIENDS

I HAVE SOME WONDERFUL FRIENDS

WHO ARE FRIENDS TO THE VERY END...

THEY BRIGHTEN AND LIGHTEN MY DAY

AND MAKE MY DAYS MORE PLESANT AND GAY...

PEN FRIENDS ARE REALLY GREAT

THEY DON'T PUT YOU DOWN AND MEDITATE...

MY FRIENDS ACCEPT ME THE WAY I AM

WE CHEER EACH OTHER UP WHEN EVER WE CAN...

EVEN THOUGH WERE FAR AWAY BY MILES

JUST A SIMPLE LETTER, LETS US SHARE LOTS OF SMILES...

WE SHARE OUR LIVES WITH EACH OTHER

BUT FEEL MORE LIKE SISTERS AND BROTHER...

WE HELP PASS AWAY THE HOURS AND TIME

OUR FRIENDSHIP IS MORE PRECIOUS THAN A GOLD MINE...

AS FAR AS MY PEN FRIENDS GO THEY ARE THE BEST

IN THE NORTH, SOUTH, EAST AND WEST...

I PRAY TO GOD TO WATCH OVER MY FRIENDS

AND I KNOW HE WILL TO THE VERY END....

28

THUNDERSTORMS

THE ROARING OF THE THUNDER

THE LIGHTING THAT COMES UNDER...

IT'S NATURES WAY

OF SHOWERING OUR DAY...

TO COOL DOWN THE CLOUDS AND AIR TOO

MAKING IT EASIER TO BREATHE FOR ME AND YOU...

THUNDERSTORMS POURS DOWN A LOT OF RAIN

SOMETIMES SOUNDS LIKE THE ROAR OR A TRAIN...

WATER IS SOMETHING, EVERYTHING NEEDS

SO GOD INVENTED THUNDERSTORMS INDEED...

AFTER THE THUNDERSTORMS GO AWAY

IT LIGHTENS AND BRIGHTENS UP THE DAY...

THEN THE BEAUTIFUL SIGHT OF THE GLOW

THE SMILE FROM GOD MAKES A RAINBOW...

OH YES I LOVE TO SEE THUNDERSTORMS

HOW IT ROARS AND MOURS...

BRINGS TOO ALL OF US PEACE AND REST

KNOWING GOD HAS DONE HIS BEST...

MOTHERS AND DAUGHTERS

MOTHERS AND DAUGHTERS ARE REALLY NEAT

THEIR QUITE PRETTY AND SWEET...

THERE SO MUCH ALIKE

IT'S HARD TO SAY WHO IS WHO AT NIGHT...

DAUGHTERS ARE REFLECTIONS OR THEIR MOTHERS

SO DIFFERENT FROM THEIR BROTHERS...

MOTHERS AND DAUGHTERS ARE QUITE UNIQUE

SWEET, CARING, GIVING AND NEAT...

DAUGHTERS FALL DOWN AND HURT THEIR KNEES

MOTHERS ARE THERE TO KEEP AWAY THE BEES...

MOTHERS AND DAUGHTERS HAVE A SPECIAL KIND OF LOVE

THAT SAILS FROM ONE ANOTHER ON A DOVE...

DAUGHTERS AND MOTHERS HAVE A SPECIAL WAY

TO KEEP SECRETS AND NOT AFRAID TO SAY...

A MOTHER HAS A SPECIAL WAY SHE KNOWS

WHAT HER DAUGHTER WILL DO AND GO...

IT'S A SPECIAL GIFT FROM GOD TO MOTHERS

TO MAKE THEIR DAUGHTERS KNOW NO OTHERS...

LIFE IS BEAUTIFUL

LIFE IS BEAUTIFUL TO THRE

WE SHOULD BE THANKFUL WE CAN SEE...

TO SMELL THE FLOWERS OR FEEL THE BREEZE

OR HEAR THE RUSTLING OF THE LEAVES...

I DON'T SMOKE AND FEEL YOUNG

MY MIND FEELS GOOD, AND SO DOES MY LUNG...

I LOVE WHAT NATURE HAS TO OFFER ME

THE ANIMALS AND MAYBE...

THE BUZZING OF THE BEES

MAKING THEIR HIVES IN THE TREES...

TAKING A WALK AT NIGHT

WITHE THE STARS SHINNING BRIGHT...

WATCHING A CHILD SMILE AND PLAY

THAT REALLY MAKES A GREAT DAY...

WATCHING CHILDREN GROW TALL

WONDERING WHAT'S IN THE FUTURE FOR THEM ALL...

LIFE IS BEAUTIFUL, LETS FRIN AND SMILE

LIFE WILL CARRY OUR THOUGHTS FOR MANY A MILE...

SOMEONE TO HOLD ME

OH HOW I WISH I HAD SOMEONES ARMS AROUND ME

TO HOLD ME, MAKE ME FEEL LOVED AND HAPPY...

NO ARMS HOLD ME ANYMORE

SINCE LOVE HAS WENT OUT THE DOOR...

LONELY I FEEL WITH NO ONE TO HOLD

JUST SIT HERE IN MY HOUSE, LONELY AND COLD...

HOW I WISH, I HAD ONE WISH TO COME TRUE

IT WOUD BE TO BE HELD FROM YOU...

DAYS, NIGHTS, WEEKS AND MONTHS ARE LONELY TOO

EVERY DAY, WVERYTHING SAME, OLD NOT NEW...

OH HOW IS WISH SOMEONE WOULD HOLD ME TIGHT

IN THE DAY TIME, OR EVEN AT NIGHT...

I SIT HERE IN MY HOME AND WAIT

FOR SOMEONE TO LOVE ME, HOLD ME AND TAKE

ME TOO BE THEIR WOMAN WHO'S TRUE

I AM WAITING AND HOPING TO LOVE ONLY YOU...

32

HAPPY MOTHERS DAY SISTER

YOU'RE THE BEST SISTER/MOTHER I KNOW

YOU TAUGHT ME RIGHT AND HELP ME TO GROW...

I COULD OF BOUGHT YOU A CARD WITH A POEM

BUT THE WORDS WOULDN'T MEAN ANYTHING LIKE MY OWN...

YOU'R MY BEST FRIEND AND PAL I EVER HAD

EVEN IF I DON'T SAY SO WHEN I AM MAD...

YOU'R ALWAYS THERE WHEN I NEED YOU TOO

BECAUSE OF THIS I LOVE YOU...

WHEN SOME DAYS I NEED TO CRY

YOU'R NOT ASKING QUESTIONS LIKE WHY...

YOU HELP ME THOUGH HEART ACKES ALL OF THE TIME

WITH LOVE IN YOUR HEART AND SMILE LIKE SUNSHINE...

IF ANYONE DESERVES A HAPPY MOTHERS DAY TOO

IT'S YOU WHO HELPS ME GET THROUGH...

THANKS FOR ALL THE THINGS YOU DONE AND DO

I AM GLAD YOUR MY SISTER AND GOD MADE YOU...

HAPPY MOTHERS DAY SISTER, OF MINE

HOPE YOU HAVE A GOOD DAY AND PLENTY OF SUNSHINE...

DIRT DON'T HURT

ASK A SMALL CHILD PLAYING IN SAND

DOES IT HURT YOUR HAND...

HE LOOKS UP AT YOU AND SAYS NO

IT FEELS GOOD ON MY TOE...

AFTER ALL GOD MADE DIRT

AND DIRT DON'T HURT...

EVERYONE NEEDS DIRT IN THEIR LIVES

DAUGHTERS, SONS, MOMS, Dads, HUSBANDS AND WIVES...

WITHOUT DIRT AROUND WE BE NEAT AND CLEAN

THAT BE BORING INSTEAD OF DIRTY AND MEAN...

WE ALL NEED TO BE A CHILD SOME DAYS

HELPS TO RELIEVE TENSION AS WE PLAY...

DIRT HELPS PLANTS TO GROW

HELPS LAWNS TO TURN GREEN AND BE MOWED...

DIRT BUILDS HOUSES, GIEANT BUILDINGS TOO

SO WE HAVE A PLACE TO LIVE FOR ME AND YOU...

GARDENS NEED DIRT TO MAKE FOOD GROW

FOR EVERYONE CANE EAT AND SO...

YES EVERYONE NEEDS FIRT IN THEIR TIME

FOR EVERY DAY NEEDS, EVERY DAY THAT'S MINE...

STARTING OVER

STARTING OVER IS SO HARD

GOT TO PROTECT AND GUARD...

YOUR HEART FROM BREAKING IN TWO

WHILE FORGETTING THE OLD AND LOOKING FOR NEW...

BREAKING UP IS HARD TO DO

WHEN YOU LOVE SOMEONE SO TRUE...

IF ONLY WE LEAVE WHAT WE CAN'T CHANGE TOO

THINGS WE CAN CHANGE, AND NOT LOOK SO BLUE...

OUR LIVES WILL GET BETTER AND BRIGHTER

DARK DAYS GO AWAY AND BECOME WHITER...

DEPRESSION WILL GO AWAY FAST

THE BAD DAYS WILL PASS...

BEFORE YOU KNOW IT, YOUR HAPPY NOT SAD

YOU'R FULL OF ENERGY, GO POWER NOT FEELING BAD...

SMILE LOTS, BE HAPPY AND HAVE FUN

THEN YOU KNOW YOU HAVE FINALLY WON...

MY DOG, MY BEST FRIEND

MY DOG IS MY BEST FRIEND

SHE WILL BE UNTIL THE END...

SHE FOLLOWS ME WHERE EVER I GO

SHE'S MY SHADOW THAT I KNOW...

SHE WAS VERY LONELY AND SAD

TILL I TOOK HER HOME, NOW SHE'S GLAD...

SHE IS MY FAVORITE PAL BY FAR

SHE LIKES TO RIDE IN MY CAR...

SHE LISTENS TO ME WHEN I TALK

AND LOVES TO GO WITH ME , TO TAKE A WALK...

SHE STICKS TO ME LIKE GLUE

THIS DOG LOVE ME TOO...

SHE STAYS CLOSE TO ME

SHE MAKES ME HAPPY...

SEEING CHILDREN AT PLAY

WATCHING CHILDREN AT PLAY

SMILING, TALKING ALL DAY...

THEY LOOK SO BRIGHT AND ALERT

AND DON'T CARE IF THEY GET HURT...

CHILDREN PLAYING IN THE SAND

MAKING A SAND CASTLE WITH THEIR HANDS...

DRIVING THERE TRUCKS OVER TO THE MILL

ONCE THEY GET OVER THE DIRT HILL...

SWINGING ON THE SWING

PRETENDING THEY ARE BIRDS WITH WINGS...

PLAYING AND SWIMMING IN THE LAKE

TILL THEY LOOK DOWN AND SEE THE SNAKE...

SNOWBALL FIGHTS ARE REALLY FUN

ESPECIALLY WITH YOUR DAUGHTER AND SON...

YES SEEING CHILDREN AT PLAY

REALLY DOES MAKE MY DAY...

SUNSHINE TO ME

I AM SO VERY GALD I CAN SEE

USE MY EYES IS THE GREATEST GIFT TO ME...

SEEING SMILES OF SUNSHINE IN THEIR FACES

THE YOUNG, THE OLD AND ALL THE PLACES...

CHILDREN RUNNING, PLAYING WITH DOGS

CATS SITTING STILL ON LOGS...

THE ELDERLY SITTING ON PARK SEATS

WATCHING AND FEEDING BIRDS THAT ARE NEAT...

HUSBANDS, WIVES, GIRLFRIENDS AND GUYS

HOLDING HANDS, AND GAZING INTO EACH OTHERS EYES...

GRANDPAS GIVING GRANDMAS A KISS

HOPING THAT'S SOMETHING THEY WONT MISS...

SINGLE MOMS PUSHING STROLLERS WITH THEIR BABE

WATCHING THEIR TODDLERS RANT AND RAVE...

SEEING AND HEARING ALL OFTHIS

KNOWING SOME DAY I TOO WILL MISS...

ALL OF THIS WHEN IT'S MY TURN TO LAY DOWN

BURRIED DEEP IN THE GROUND...

BUT FOR RIGHT NOW I WILL SMELL THE ROSES AND AIR

AND BE THANKFUL I AM THERE...

TO SMELL, TOUCH AND SEE

AND TO BE JUST OLE ME...

THE RAINBOW

OH HOW I WONDER HOW IT IS UNDER THE RAINBOW

DOES THE POT OF GOLD REALLY GLOW...

IS LIFE FAST OR IS IT SLOW

UNDER NEATH THE RAINBOW...

I WOULD LIKE TO FOLLOW IT SOME DAY

IF ONLY I COULD FIND A WAY...

I THINK THAT LIFE WOULD BE MUCH BRIGHTER

MUCH BETTER, BEAUTIFUL AND LIGHTER...

THAT PEOPLE WOULD NEVER HAVE TO BE SAD

BUT ALL THE TIME SINGING AND GLAD...

OH HOW I WISH I COULD SLIMB THE RAINBOW

AND FILL MY MEMORIES UP IN A BOWL...

THAT I COULD KEEP IN MY MIND FOREVER

AND NO ONE COULD STEAL FROM ME NEVER...

THAT KIND OF LIFE WOULD BE GREAT FOR ME

AS I COULD FEEL LIKE THE BIRDS OF THE SEA...

OH YES IF I COULD GO TO THE RAINBOW

I WOULD BE ABLE TO SEE THE GOLD GLOW...

BUT AT THIS TIME I CAN'T CLIMB UP THERE

SO FOR NOW, I WILL BE CONTENT ON EARTH DOWN HERE...

MY SISTER

I HAVE A WONDERFUL SISTER YOU SEE

GOD CREATED HER JUST FOR ME...

WHEN EVER I AM HAVING A HARD TIME

SHE'S THERE AND NEVER ASKS FOR A DIME...

MY SISTER ISN'T JUST MY SIS, SHE'S MY BEST FRIEND

SHE WILL STAY THAT WAY TO THE VERY END...

I MAY BE THE BIGGEST AND TALLEST

BUT SHE'S THE GREATEST, EVEN IF THE SMALLEST...

LIVING LIFE WITHOUT MY SIS WOULD BE LIVING HELL

SO THERE FOR I DON'T THINK MUCH OF IT AND DWELL...

MY SISTER HAS A GREAT PERSONALITY AND SMILES

THAT CARRIES ONES THOUGHTS FOR MANY MILES...

YOU HAVE TURNED MY RAINY DAYS INTO SUNSHINE

YOU BEING MY SIS, IS WORTH THAN A GOLD MINE...

SISTER PLEASE LISTEN TO ME

I LOVE YOU VERY MUCH YOU SEE...

YOU HAVE HELPED ME MORE THAN ANYONE

I WANT TO THANK YOU FOR EVERYTHING YOU HAVE DONE...

AS I CLOSE THIS POEM I LIKE TO SAY

I THANK GOD FOR YOU EVERY SINGLE DAY...

STARS

HOW TINY THE STARS LOOK AT NIGHT

IN THE SKY SO DARK NOT LIGHT...

THEY TWINKLE LIKE GEMS IN THE SKY

DO YOU WONDER HOW AND WHY...

I BELIEVE THE STARS ARE OF PEOPLE WHO PASSED AWAY

WHO NOW SMILES ON US AND WANT TO STAY...

I LOVE THE STAR FILLED SKIES AT NIGHT

THE STARS LIGHT UP THE SKY SO BRIGHT...

ONE DAY I WILL BE A STAR UP THERE TOO

SHINNING DOWN WITH A SMILE FOR YOU...

A SINGLE MOMS DAY

EACH AND EVERY DAY WE WAKE

TO START A NEW DAY AND MAKE...

THE BEST OF WHAT WE CAN DO

TO HELP OURSELVES AND OTHERS TOO...

BREAKFAST TO MAKE, CHILDREN TO RISE

GET THEM TO SCHOOL, SO THEY CAN BE WISE...

HURRY, HUSTLE AND BUSTLE TO WORK FOR

HOPING OUR BOSSES WON'T YELL THROUGH THE DOOR...

THE CHILDREN NEED SHOES, CLOTHING AND BOOKS

HURRY THROUGH THE STORE AND GET DIRTY LOOKS...

THE CHILDREN ARE YELLING, THE BABY MAY CRY

DO YOU EVER WONDER WHY YOU TRY...

HURRY HOME ALMOST BEDTIME FOR THE CHILDREN

YOU'RE EVEN TOO TIRED TO GRIN...

SUPPER TO MAKE, CHILDREN TO FEED

A FRIEND STOPS BY TO ASK FOR A GOOD DEED...

AT THE END OF THE DAY, YOU LAY DOWN AND PRAY

HOPING TOMORROW IS A BETTER DAY...

LOSING SOMEONE CLOSE TO YOU

LOSING SOMEONE CLOSE TO YOU

MAKES YOU DEPRESSED, SAD AND BLUE...

IT'S HARD TO JUST LET THEM GO

SAYING GOOD BYE AND SO...

JUST THINK OF THE HAPPINESS YOU HAD

WITH THE PERSON THAT'S DIED AND MADE YOU SAD...

THAT SOMEONE CLOSE WOULD WANT YOU TO BE

CARE FREE, HAPPY GO ON WITH LIFE AND SEE...

THERE IN HEAVEN NOW WITH GOD

NOT JUST BURIED UNDER THE SOD...

THERE LOOKING DOWN AND GUIDING YOU

SO YOU WILL ONCE AGAIN, BE HAPPY TOO...

YOU MUST LET THE DEPARTED GO

START YOUR LIFE OVER YOU KNOW...

NEVER LET YOUR MEMORIES ESCAPE YOU

JUST LET THAT SOMEONE, BE AT REST TOO...

HOLD ONTO

HOLD ONTO YOUR LITTLE ONES

ALWAYS BUCKLE UP YOUR DAUGHTERS AND SONS...

THEIR LIVES ARE FRAGILE AND DEAR

WITH SEAT BELTS ON, MOMS AND DADS WONT CRY A TEAR...

IT ONLY TAKES A SECOND TO WIPE OUT THEIR LIVES TOO

SO HOLD ONTO THEM SO THEY CAN LOVE YOU...

NO STANDING UP ON THE SEAT

OR SOMEONE WILL WIND UP AND WEEP...

SO HOLD ONTO YOUR BUNDLE OF JOY AND PRIDE

MAKE THEM SAFE FOR A NICE LONG RIDE...

SUMMER IS

SUMMER IS THE PLACE TO BE

BARBECUES, VACATIONS AND THE SEA...

EATING WATERMELON WITH A GRIN

WONDERING IF YOU CAN GET IT DONE AND WIN...

PIC NICS ON A BLANKET ON THE GROUND

WATCHING FOR THE ANTS TO COME AROUND...

ICE COLD SODA TO QUENCH THE THIRST

GETTING A SUNBURN THAT'S THE WORSE...

SWIM SHORTS, BATHING SUITS, POPSICKLES TOO

FOR EVERYONE TO KEEP COOL FOR ME AND YOU...

SITTING ON THE BEACH IN THE SUN

WATCHING PEOPLE GO BY ONE BY ONE...

ICE CHEST, FISHING POLES AND BAIT

NOW TO SIT BACK AND WAIT...

CANOEING, BOATING ON THE LAKE

TILL YOUR SO TIRED ALL YOU DO IS ACHE...

WATCHING SPIDERS MAKE A WEB

OR HEARING THE ECHO OF AN EBB...

LEAVES THAT TURN GREEN, LAWNS THAT GROW

GARDENS ARE PLANTED ALL IN A ROW...

THIS IS WHAT SUMMER IS TO ME

THIS ALL MAKES ME HAPPY...

CAN'T GET AHEAD

EVER HAVE THOSE DAYS THAT YOU CAN'T GET AHEAD

NO MATTER WHAT YOU DO, NO MATTER WHAT YA SAID...

THOSE DAYS TRAIL BEHIND US A LOT

WHETHER WE LIKE IT OR NOT...

THE MORE WE TRY THE LESS WE GET TOO

SOME DAYS WHY DO WE TRY AS NOTHING IS NEW...

WE GO TO WORK AND SLAVE ALL DAY

TO GET THE MONEY FOR OUR PAY...

TO PAY BILLS EACH WEEK

AND HAVE NO MONEY NOW THAT'S NOT NEAT...

OR HAVE ONE OF THOSE DAYS YOU WASH YOUR CAR

SO THE NEXT DAY THEY PAVE THE ROAD WITH TAR...

AND THEN WHEN YOU THINK YOUR GETTING AHEAD

THE NEXT DAY YOU FIND YOUR CAR BATTERY IS DEAD...

ONE CAN'T GET AHEAD THESE DAYS IT SEEMS

NO MATTER IF YOUR GOOD, BAD OR MEAN...

SO WE SHOULD TAKE ONE DAY AT A TIME

MAYBE SOME LUCK WILL COME AROUND LIKE A GOLD MINE...

NATURE

I LOVE TO BE WITH THE WILD THINGS

THE FLOWERS, THE TREES, THE BIRDS THAT SING...

TO HEAR THE CRICKETS PLAY THEIR TUNE

AT NIGHT UNDER THE MOON...

THE FIRE FLIES THAT LIGHT UP THE SKY

HAVE YOU EVER WONDERED HOW AND WHY...

THE FLICKER OF THE MOON ACROSS A LAKE

OH HOW I LOVE TO STAY UP AND AWAKE...

THOSE PESKY RACCOONS LOOKING FOR FOOD

THE WAY THEY WRESTLE, WHEN IN THE MOOD...

OH HOW I LOVE NATURE TOO

IT'S A GIFT FROM GOD FOR ME AND YOU...

SIMBA

SIMBA IS MY SIAMESE CAT

WHO I SWEAR HAS WINGS LIKE A BAT...

HE RUNS DOWN THE HALL AT NIGHT

JUMPING FROM WALL TO WALL, AS IF IN FLIGHT...

HE'S A BEAUTIFUL FAT OLD CAT

WHO LIKES TO PLAY WITH YOUR CAP...

HE CURLS UP INTO A BALL ON YOUR LAP

SO HE CAN GET COMFORTABLE AND TAKE A NAP...

CAT'S MAKE A PERFECT PET

THEY TAKE CARE OF THEMSELVES, AND GO IN THEIR
BOXES TO WET...

SIMBA LIKES TO PLAY SOMETIMES

I AM GLAD HE'S ALL MINE...

THE TOUCHES OF TIME

WHAT DOES TIME REALLY MEAN TO US

BESIDES LIVING IN FLESH, BODY AND NOT DUST...

TIME USING OUR ENERGY AND BRAIN

HELPS US LIVE AND BE TRAINED...

IT HELPS US TO LIVE FULFILLING LIVES

MARRING AND BECOMING HUSBANDS AND WIVES...

TAKING TIME TO REPRODUCE MINI'S OF US

TO HELP THE WORLD GROW AND NOT TURN TO RUST...

THE SMILING FACES WE SEE EACH DAY

FROM STRANGERS, THE POOR AND ALL WHO STAY...

THESE ARE TOUCHES OF TIME

ANYTHING THAT BRINGS LAUGHTER, LOVE AND SUNSHINE...

DRUNKS

DO DRUNKS REALLY KNOW WHAT THEY DO

BEHIND THE STEERING WHEEL THEY KNEW...

THEIR EYES ARE BLURRED FROM ALL THE DRINKS

CAN THEY SEE A CHILD IN FRONT OF THEM WHO WINKS...

THEIR REACTION IS SLOWED DOWN REAL FAR

FROM ALL THE DRINKS THEY HAD AT THE BAR...

THEY CAN'T HARDLY WALK TOO

SO WHY GET BEHIND THE WHEEL, AND DRIVE FROM YOU...

DRUNKS ARE VERY SICK INSIDE

THEY DESTROY THEMSELVES AND OTHERS AS THEY RIDE...

NO ONE CAN TELL DRUNKS THEY HAD ENOUGH TOO

THEY THINK THEY KNOW MORE THAN YOU...

EVEN THOUGH THEY CAN'T SPEAK

THEY STAND UP AS IF THEIR WEAK...

THEY STILL FEEL THEY ARE IN CONTROL OF THEIR SELVES

EVEN WHEN THEY WET ALL OVER THEM SELVES...

STOP COVERING UP THOSE GLASSES

TAKE HOLD OF YOUR LIFE AND STOP ACTING LIKE ASSES...

FACE THE PROBLEMS ALL OF YOU HAVE

DON'T COVER THEM UP AND FELL BAD...

COVERING THEM UP WITH DRINKS KILLS A LIFE

IT COULD BE YOUR DAUGHTER, YOUR SON OR YOUR WIFE???

GET HELP BEFORE IT'S TO LATE

DON'T PUT IT OFF FOR YOUR OWN SAKE...

LIFE IS GREAT, LIFE IS GOOD, LIFE IS BRIGHT

STOP DRINKING AND DRIVING AND SAVE A PERSONS LIFE...

WHY DOES MY HEART GO

WHY DOES MY HEART GO ON BEATING

WHY DOES MY LOVE GO ON...

IT'S ALL BECAUSE OF A MAN CALLED BABE

THAT KEEPS IT GOING STRONG...

IT'S AMAZING WHAT ONE MAN CAN DO

TO EASE THE MIND AND SET A NEW...

AND MELT THE COLD INTO CREAM

MAKING ME FEEL JUST LIKE A QUEEN...

I WOULDN'T TRADE YOU

FOR ANYONE NEW...

NOT FOR ANY AMOUNT OF MONEY

BECAUSE YOU'RE MY HONEY...

NATURE AND ME

I WAS BORN TO LIVE IN THE COUNTRY

TO SEE THE ANIMALS AND HEAR THE BIRDS IN THE TREE...

NATURE IS WHERE I NEED TO BE

SO I CAN FEEL SO FREE, FREE, FREE...

BEING COUPED UP IN THIS TRAILER HOME

MAKES ME FEEL SO ALL ALONE...

BEING WITH NATURE AND WILD THINGS

MAKES ME FEEL LIKE I CAN FLY AND HAVE WINGS...

I WILL SEEK, LOOK, HOPE, DREAM AND MORE

FOR MY HOME IN THE COUNTRY WITH THE BIG WOOD DOOR...

DREAMS

EVERYONE NEEDS A DREAM

TO MAKE LIFE FLOW EASY DOWN A STREAM...

DREAMS ARE EXCITING TO PLAN FOR

TO OPEN UP OUR MINDS AND LOTS, LOTS MORE...

MY DREAM IS TO BE IN THE COUNTRY

TO WRITE MY BOOKS UNDER NEATH THE TREE...

TO SMELL THE WILD FLOWERS, AND WATCH THEM GROW

OR SEE ALL THE VEGETABLES ALL IN A ROW...

TO WATCH WILD ANIMALS SEARCH FOR FOOD TOO

OR HEAR THE COWS GO MOO-MOO-MOO...

HAVING THE SUNLIGHT SHINE DOWN ON ME

GLITTERING IN THE WATER FOR EVERYONE TO SEE...

BULLFROGS CROAKING AND CRICKETS SINGING

LISTENING TO THE CHURCH BELLS RINGING...

LIVING OFF THE LAND LIKE THE GOOD OLE TIMES

AND KNOWING IT'S ALL MINE, MINE, MINE...

GODS SPECIAL CHILD

YOU CAN SEE I CAN'T DO MUCH ANYMORE

I'M GETTING WEAKER, AND I CAN'T WALK OUT THE DOOR...

MY EYES AREN'T SO BRIGHT

BUT I CAN STILL SEE DAY LIGHT...

MY HAIR HAS GONE ASTRAY

BUT I FEEL FINE TODAY...

MY HANDS DON'T WORK WELL THESE DAYS

AS LONG AS I CAN HOLD HANDS, THAT'S ALL THAT
MATTERS ANYWAYS...

MY PARENTS ARE SO WONDERFUL AND DEAR

ESPECIALLY RIGHT NOW, THAT THEY ARE NEAR...

MY TINY LIFE IS EASING AWAY FAST

ONE DAY OR NIGHT I WILL PASS...

ONCE I HAVE WENT AWAY WITH GOD

I WANT MY PARENTS TO SMILE AND NOD...

KNOWING THAT GOD MAKES SPECIAL PEOPLE TOO

THAT'S WHY GOD MADE ME, JUST TO LOVE YOU...

I WILL LOOK DOWN FROM HEAVEN AND SAY

PLEASE GOD, TAKE CARE OF MY PARENTS TODAY...

UNTIL THE DAY, THEY TO COME HOME

THEN WE WILL BE TOGETHER AND NEVER ALONE...

BYE MOM

MOM I WILL MISS YOU MUCH

ESPECIALLY MISS HOW YOU LOOK AND TOUCH...

THOSE LOVING ARMS THAT HELP ME GET THROUGH

IN GOOD TIMES, BAD, OLD AND NEW...

THE SPECIAL WAY YOU HELPED US ALL

NO MATTER IF WE WERE RICH, POOR, SHORT, OR TALL...

THAT SPECIAL SMILE OF LOVE

IS GONE WITH GOD NOW ON A DOVE...

YOU MADE PEOPLE HAPPY HERE ON EARTH

NOW IT'S TIME TO DO SO IN HEAVEN IT'S WORTH...

I MUST LET YOU GO NOW SO I CAN

LEARN TO LIVE MY LIFE AGAIN...

YOU DONE EVERYTHING HERE ON EARTH

YOU MADE MANY PEOPLE HAPPY SINCE YOUR BIRTH...

EVEN THOUGH YOU'RE GONE

MY LOVE FOR YOU WILL GO ON AND ON...

" LOVE YOU MOM"